Mindfulness for

Everyday Mindfuln
Enjoy Your Life, Be Happy, Reduce Stress and Create Freedom

By Marta Tuchowska

Copyright © 2015 by Marta Tuchowska

www.holisticwellnessproject.com

www.amazon.com/author/mtuchowska

All rights reserved. No part of this publication may be reproduced, stored in a retrieval system, or transmitted, in any form or by any means, electronic, mechanical, photocopying, recording or otherwise, without the prior written permission of the author and the publishers.

All information in this book has been carefully researched and checked for factual accuracy. However, the author and publishers make no warranty, expressed or implied, that the information contained herein is appropriate for every individual, situation or purpose, and assume no responsibility for errors or omission. The reader assumes the risk and full responsibility for all actions, and the author will not be held liable for any loss or damage, whether consequential, incidental, special or otherwise that may result from the information presented in this publication. By purchasing this book you have agreed to the aforementioned statement.

TABLE OF CONTENTS

From the Author...6

Free Audio Book + Guided Meditation...15

Mindfulness Tips for Busy People:

Tip # 1 You Are Awake...16

Tip # 2 Another Day of Your Beautiful Life...17

Tip # 3 Enjoy the Process of Waking Up Your Amazing Body...17

Tip # 4 Create Your Morning Ritual: full-time, part-time, and limited time options...18

Tip #5 Mindful Body and Mind Refreshment: shower of good energy...20

Tip #6 Sip on Your Favorite Drink and Let All Your Cells Be Dancing for You...21

Tip #7 Your Mind Loves Mindfulness. Give It a Natural High!...21

Tip #8 Mindfulness and Positivity Through Journaling...22

Tip #9 Mindful Planning without Over- Planning...24

Tip #10 Mindful Affirmations...25

Tip #11 Mindful Natural High Moments...27

Tip #12 Work Routine Made Exciting and Fun...31

Tip #13 Commuting or Driving to Work. What's the Stress All About?...32

Tip #14 Mindful Short and Sweet Breaks...33

Tip #15 Work to Live, Not the Other Way Round- Be Holistically Productive...38

Tip #16 Stay Nice and Fresh...42

Tip #17 Mindful Eating...43

Tip #18 Mindful Waiting (cut off your fingers)...45

Tip #19 The Best Mindfulness Drug - Music...47

Tip #20 Change Your Mood with Aromas- Mindfulness Spiced Up...47

Tip #21 Smile- It's Free!...48

Tip #22 Mindful Holistic Self-Massage...49

Tip #23 Mindful Anxiety Relief...54

Tip #24 Mindful Communication ...55

Tip #25 Create Positive Energy around You...57

Tip #26 How to Create Natural Caffeine Boost with Mindfulness...58

Tip #27 Make Things Simple (technology)...60

Tip #28 Mindfulness and Balance (how to achieve personal and professional success)...62

Tip #29 Fall in Love with Fitness- a Few Mindfulness Tricks That Can Help...65

Tip #30 Your Holistic Health Spa at Home and Mindfulness...67

Tip #31 Go Out and Have Fun- How to Practice Mindfulness in a Night Club...68

Tip #32 Mindfulness and Self-Healing...70

Tip #33 Mindfulness and Goal Setting (Mindful Vision)...72

Tip #34 Mindfulness and Motivation...72

Tip #35 Mindfulness and Self-Coaching Questions...74

Tip #36 Your Evening/ Night Ritual...75

Tip #37 Breathe and Just Be Yourself...75

Tip #38 Mindfulness and Nature...77

Tip #39 Be Like a Little Kid...79

Conclusion...81

Connect with Marta...85

From the Author

Dear Reader,

Thank you so much for stopping by and taking an interest in my book. It really means a lot to me. My goal is to give you some really simple and practical tips to help you create more emotional freedom, wellbeing, focus, and enjoyment, even if you are the busiest person in the universe.

The first thing I would like to embark on is the very definition of mindfulness and how it is perceived in this day and age. Let me ask you this question: what comes to your mind when you hear or see the word 'mindfulness'? Or what do you think would crop up if you search for it on Google Images, Flickr, or Pinterest? You and I both know that it would probably be a bunch of inspiring pictures with someone like a peaceful person meditating or doing yoga. In most cases it would be a young girl doing yoga.

Now, don't get me wrong. I love those pictures, they help me create nice, warm feelings of wellness almost immediately. However, there is also a drawback. You see, many people would say, "Oh right, mindfulness is like a yoga meditation thing and I don't have time to do it as much as I would love to." We also need to realize that this is the idea that media and mainstream marketing creates- it's a perfect hook for expensive seminars and retreats. By the way, I love retreats and seminars, I have absolutely nothing against them. They can lead to a massive progress in health and personal growth. What I am saying is that an average 21st century individual with a job, business, family, or other obligations such as college, doesn't have time to get involved in retreats every day, right?

Retreats and seminars are amazing for holidays and weekends, however we should not postpone our wellness 'till we finally get some time off. We need a simple step-by-step walkthrough so that we can design an easy routine that will improve our simple everyday mindfulness that, as the name suggests, can be done every single day. From the moment you open your eyes while you're still in bed, 'till when you go back to bed again. You can even use mindfulness to fight insomnia, communicate with your subconscious mind, and simply to have nice dreams.

So here comes my definition of mindfulness. By the way, you may agree or disagree with me, you can even only agree with me partially. Our different opinions is what makes us special, I am not here to argue that what I say is right. We are all right. You are right, when you create something that works for your own body and mind. Listening to your body is always right. Sharing your experiences with other people so that they can create healthier lifestyles is always right.

Mindfulness is the art of living in the here and now and being utterly grateful for this very special moment. It's the art of appreciation of everything around you and simply listening and tuning in. It's working on all your senses and embracing this moment. Since you are alive, you can practice mindfulness all day long and even all night long if you want to. It doesn't matter if you are working, talking to a friend, working out, reading, or playing with your kids.

Just focus on this moment. Focus on one thing. Let the rest go. When the time is right, you will focus on the rest of your day. What you really need to focus on right now is reading this very book. Your mind may start wandering, after all, you need to do this and that, and there are so many other books you want to read. I totally understand. I always get that feeling when I look at some of the new books waiting for me on my Kindle device. I wish I could read them all at once. At some point, I would just skim through all the books I ordered because I wanted to read certain amount of books per month. Now I actually use another approach. Again, don't get me wrong, I have nothing against speed-reading. I am sure that one can practice speed-reading and mindfulness at the same time. What I want you to focus on is your precious time. Whilst some people want to magically create more time that they can use to try to seem busy or preoccupied, what I suggest you start training your mind to is ***intensify*** *the time that you have.*

Even if you believe you don't have enough free time, focus on what you have and intensify it. For example, you can read just one book and take your time and let the information and inspiration soak into every cell of your beautiful body. This can help you feel much more relaxed than trying to be a superhuman who tries to devour 5 books at once. Remember, there is time for everything. In this day and age, there is way too much information and we need to be selective. Less is better. You can do less, but with more focus. This will give you the feeling that you actually have more time. And feeling that way will make you less anxious. You will still be active, but there will be less stress and less rushing around. All you need to do now is to be slightly more selective. Ok, I am not talking about *just* books. I actually used the example of reading as a metaphor. Think about it next time when you create your to-do lists. I understand that it will not always be possible, but just try to remember to go for the "less is more" rule.

Time is usually the biggest issue that prevents people from achieving their health and fitness goals. As a wellness coach, I'm very often asked about a whole variety of topics from nutrition to meditation, motivation, and even productivity. I believe it's all interconnected- body, mind, and spirit. All systems must go. By picking up this book, you have made a commitment of becoming more mindful and therefore more grateful. Mindfulness is also focus and productivity.

My first suggestion is that you stop saying, "I don't have time," or "I am busy." Now, there is nothing wrong with that. I am busy myself. Everyone is. However, I have noticed, both from my own experiences as well as my clients' and even some of my friends', that as soon as you start saying:

- "I am active but stress-free!"

- "I enjoy every minute of all my activities, they make me feel ALIVE and grateful   for the present moment!"

- "I am busy, but in a holistic way. I work on my body, mind, and spirit and I love it!"

- "I lead an active lifestyle doing things I am really passionate about."

Some really amazing things will begin to happen in your life. You will be able to shift your mindset from the grumpy, *"I am busy, not now. I am stressed out,"* point to a more empowering, *"I am active but stress-free, this is what makes me feel alive."* Thanks to that, you will be able to create more energy in your life and develop a more positive outlook.

This is actually a combination of NLP (Neuro-Linguistic Programming) and mindfulness techniques. Talk to yourself, feel it, and live it. All you need to do is to focus on the now. The rest can, and will, wait.

I can still remember myself from a few years ago. I was already on my journey to wellness, and I was looking for something to improve my wellbeing by releasing anxiety. I got quite interested in yoga and meditation and would try to have a regular practice, but I was still a bit of a mess. I just forgot one really important thing: practices such as yoga and meditation should also take place outside of yoga mats and meditation cushions. This was a lesson I learned thanks to one of my old roommates. I can still remember what he said in his melodic Argentinean Spanish. By the way, I love it when they pronounce the "y" sound as "sch".

You need to do yoga not only in the yoga class, but also in your life in general. Also talking to me, reading a book or even cleaning.

From that moment on, something had changed in my life and I decided to focus on the inside. I would like to add that I am not perfect, I am not a spiritual guru. I am not pretending to be one. I am a modern, 21st century girl. I am a seeker just like you. My mission is to come up with as many natural and holistic tools that I can so that I can help other people achieve their wellness and self-growth goals. I also want the tools to be practical and easy to apply.

In the last few years, I have undergone quite a few transformations that have actually led me to big personal and professional changes. From then on I had no choice but keep researching and living my holistic wellness mission. I wanted to know how I could create my sacred mindfulness rituals that actually worked so that I could share them with other people. What also inspires me a lot are questions I get from my readers, blog followers, clients, and friends. I see myself both as a student and a teacher. I can learn from you and you can learn from me.

Do you know what I really love about mindfulness? It's free and there are no contraindications really! I love all natural types of therapy, for example herbs and aromatherapy, but mindfulness is just a killer. As long as you master it, you'll have it for the rest of your life and it will actually work for you and your wellness. Mindfulness will help you achieve better results in your personal and professional life. Just the other day, I got an e-mail from an author who wanted to know my productivity secret. It's simple- focus and mindfulness.

The rituals I describe in this book have helped me take my passion to the next level and they can help you as well. When I write, I switch off my mobile. I tell all my friends and people I work with I will be away for a while. They usually know that it means one thing- Marta is writing a new book! It's only me, music, aromatherapy, my thoughts, and the tremendous amounts of joy that I constantly escalate just by embracing mindfulness.

Just to let you know, it's natural high. People utilize different drugs and substances to achieve this state, but it's not necessary. Our brain can produce tons of natural chemicals that will help you achieve the state of natural ecstasy. This is mindfulness. This is your new, all-natural drug. It's free, it's healthy, you cannot overdose on it, and there are no side effects. Oh well, there you are. You can get too happy and too excited, but I don't think that is a problem really.

This book is a short and sweet manual that is designed to help you to slow down, even if 'technically' you can't create more hours in your life. The trick is to enjoy the hours that you spend on just being alive, awake, active, and aware. You don't have to wait 'till you finish work or go on vacation. You can start practicing right now. For example, before you start reading a new book, whether it's this one or something else, tell your mind:

"Wow, it's amazing, I can have a private conversation with this author! I can absorb all their thoughts and learn from them. Reading makes me feel relaxed. This is why I can always find 5 minutes a day for mindful reading!"

Remember, whatever it is that you do, do it from the point of confidence and relaxation. Don't do it from the standpoint of, "I have to" or, "I gotta do it quick." It's better to do things with a clear purpose of enjoyment and freedom. You can give yourself this gift now. Even if you are reading this book on a bus, subway, or a busy train.

If you are at home, you can even create a ritual to accompany it. Aromatherapy candles or a diffuser, and some nice music, which depending on your mood can be some soft yoga music, ambient, or chill, or maybe you want some lounge-house music with a more energetic beat- it's up to you. It's only you and your mind. And of course, since you are reading this book, it's me as well. Of course, you can always switch me off if you don't like me.

You have all the time in the world. You can relax. Breathe in and out deeply and slowly, whatever feels right for you.

Instead of complaining that you are busy, try to say:

- "I love working, it makes me a better person. I feel alive!"

- "My active schedule and mindfulness go hand in hand."

- "I create new, empowering, mindful habits as much as I can but I also allow myself some margins to get off track."

Whenever you have a break from work, even if it's only a 5 minute break to have a coffee, tea, or whatever it might be, instead of thinking:

"Heck, I still have to do this and that, will this hell never end?"

Focus on your break and your drink. Say:

-"Wow, this tastes fantastic. I love it. It's amazing, it's beautiful!"

Mindfulness is also about embracing positivity as much as you can. This is how you can actually purify your energy field even if you don't have time to sit on a meditation cushion and do some more sophisticated chakra rituals. I mean you certainly can, but if you don't have time, it's still fine since you can do some other stuff and feel amazing. We'll discuss that later.

So my friend, this rather lengthy intro should give you an idea of what we are just about to explore. Take your time and don't forget to practice what you have learned. This book is mostly designed for busy people, but to be honest everyone is welcome here. It doesn't matter if you work full time, part time, overtime, no time, or are currently off. Mindfulness serves to enhance our quality of life. It doesn't matter what we do or where we are. You can be mindful and happy in your office or workplace. Just like you could be down at the beach, but unmindful and letting your mind control you. Mindfulness is about appreciation and feeling alive. My goal is to make you feel joyful and positive with each paragraph that you read. The rest will be your creation. I do 1% of the work for you. Then you also do 1%, and mindfulness will do the rest for you. Isn't that amazing?

Thanks again for taking an interest in my book. In appreciation, I would love to offer you the audio version of this book + complimentary guided meditation for free.

DOWNLOAD LINK:

www.holisticwellnessproject.com/mindfulness-audiobook/giveaway.html

As an added bonus, I will also send you a free copy of my book "Holistically Productive" (PDF and MOBI formats).

Tip # 1 You Are Awake

Your commitment to mindfulness should start first thing in the morning, as soon as you open your eyes. I know it sounds a bit preachy, but trust me, after following your favorite mindfulness tips from this book, you will have a much easier time waking up early and you'll actually enjoy it. Think about it. What's the first thing that comes to your mind when you wake up? In my case, it used to be a whole range of unpleasant thoughts like: "Oh no, I have to get up, oh no, I don't feel like doing this and that." As you can guess, those thoughts would lead me to anxious states. It wasn't until I discovered a few mindfulness and gratitude tricks that things began to change.

What I do now and what I really recommend you start doing is very simple. The first thing you need to do when you open your beautiful eyes is to smile. Have a look around your bedroom, or wherever it is that you are sleeping and smile. When you smile, there is no place for worry, anger, or anxiety. Smile and be grateful that you are alive. Be grateful for all your senses. It's a miracle. Life is a miracle. Most people get up thinking, "Heck, it's another Monday!", or "What's the point of doing this and that if I can stay in bed," or "Man, I am so tired!"

Guess what? If you keep saying that, this is what your mind will believe. You need to wane off negativity with smiling, gratitude, and positive thoughts. Feel the softness of your bed and the pillows under your head. Take a few deep breaths. Observe your body. It's telling you it wants to get up and move. It will suffer if you decide to stay in bed longer than it needs.

Tip # 2 Another Day of Your Beautiful Life

Most people say they don't have time to meditate. However, when you become mindful, you do meditation while you're still in bed getting ready to get up. Keep the smile on your face and say to yourself, "I am alive. I want to celebrate it." Take a few deep breaths. Imagine all the cells of your body, getting more and more of the oxygen they so desperately need. Your body has been asleep for many hours, and now it needs some kind of refreshment and movement so that it can wake up and work for you. You don't need to wait 'till you get your cup of coffee or tea. In fact, the more you practice mindfulness first thing in the morning, the less you will feel like using caffeine to wake you up.

Tip # 3 Enjoy the Process of Waking Up Your Amazing Body

Now, start stretching your body. Make sure you keep your eyes open so as to not fall asleep again. Move your left leg, and then the right leg. Flex and stretch your feet and ankles. Lie on your stomach and gently lift your arms. Keep moving and stretching. Finally, sit on the edge of your bed and stretch again. Move your arms and head. Observe your body. Don't rush. How does it feel to take your time and wake it up naturally?

The main focus here should be listening to your body and observing it. The more you practice, the more tricks you will discover. You will be able to confront the day feeling happier and stronger. Remember to use your smile as a weapon. Observe what happens when you smile and what happens when you forget to smile. Which do you prefer? Honestly, I prefer to smile. Now, grab a glass of water and hydrate all your cells. It may be a good idea to make sure you always have some fresh water on your nightstand.

Stretch again, and finally get up. You may even start jumping around- when you move your body, it acts as a natural lymphatic drainage that stimulates your lymphatic system, which is like a sewage system in your body that helps you get rid of toxins.

Again, it may take some time to develop this mindful 'wake up and get up' habit, but with practice and repetition, you will master it and you'll actually wonder how you could ever live without it. How you start your day is how your end your day. Of course, if you have time, you could also incorporate some yoga or meditation to really take it to the next level. However, I assume that most of you readers are busy and are looking for quick solutions.

The most important thing to learn is to be more aware of your body, as well as your thoughts. When you smile, it's really hard to surrender to negative thoughts and feelings .When you smile, your inner energy changes and so does your physiology.

Tip # 4 Create Your Morning Ritual: full-time, part-time, and limited time options

Successful people always make sure that they start their day in a proactive way. Think about it- most people complain they don't have enough time. However, you already know that the best thing to do is to take advantage of the time that you already have. Yes! Time is the most limited resource. However, if you manage to take some of it and give it to the most important person on the planet (which is you), you will get peace of mind and a sense of happiness. You need to create your simple and mindful rituals first thing in the morning. Think about them as your new habits that help you unleash the power of mindfulness.

This is something that Tony Robbins refers to as your 'hour of power'. However, I recognize that very few people could find an hour to go through their morning rituals. What you should focus on to begin with are just 5 minutes. Simply pick up one mindful activity and stick to it. This could be meditation, or dancing around to your favorite music. It could be also reading a book or doing yoga. Simply choose one thing and do it for 5 minutes every morning. If you can do more, great!

I very often get asked what I do as my morning ritual, so I guess you might be asking me that question right now. First of all, I always make sure that I change things and my rituals so as not to get bored. Also, many things depend on the season. For example, in the summer, I like to go outside and do a short yoga session on my patio. I usually get up really early, so it's not too hot. It's the perfect time to tune in and wake up my body and mind. I usually do it for 15 minutes. In the winter however, I like to do a quick, energetic workout at home. Again, it's only 15 minutes. I create a playlist out of my favorite songs that give me natural energy. While moving my body, I observe how it gradually wakes up and how good it feels to be alive and to move it. Again, this is not what I call a full athletic workout. The purpose of my morning ritual is to basically feel the body and mind connection and to be ready to start the day in my peak state. I really recommend you pick up something like a quick workout, yoga, stretching, or even dancing and do it for about 10 minutes every day. A short walk if you have time could also be great. You can observe how your city or town gradually wakes up. Tune in. Listen and smile...

By the way, feel free to arrange the following tips any way you wish. You may also skip some of them or simply play around and create your own mindfulness schedule depending on your time, mood, and day.

Tip #5 Mindful Body and Mind Refreshment: shower of good energy

Your morning shower can also be a great mindfulness practice. You can stimulate relaxation with some nice music and aromatherapy. You can think of your bathroom as a luxurious spa, and feel as if you were on a holiday. Many people wait 'till a holiday or vacation because they want to experience the feelings of relaxation and happiness. However, you can feel happy and relaxed now. You don't need to wait. Breathe in and observe. Intensify your morning ritual time. Water wakes up your body and it also helps you get rid of negativity. Think of it as a shower of good energy that helps you balance your chakras and cleanse your auras. Also, be grateful for the luxury of having a shower. There are many people in the world who can't even dream about it. Instead of thinking of what you need to get done today, say to your subconscious, "I am relaxing now. I deserve it, it feels so good!"

Focus on the temperature of water and the fragrance of your soap. Pick up some gentle, natural skin scrub and think of it as emotional peeling. Be here and now. Even if you don't have time, you still need to find some time somewhere to have a shower, right? So why not be mindful about it and add it to your holistic relaxation kit?

Tip #6 Sip on Your Favorite Drink and Let All Your Cells Be Dancing for You

Most people grab their morning coffee or some other drink and just consume it in a rush following the 'as fast as you can' rule. However, you are now committed to mindfulness, so you want to take those pretty normal and everyday moments, embrace them, and transform them into something unusual. Create a ritual around your morning drink. For example, in the winter I love some nice warm chai tea. While the water is boiling, I touch and smell the teabags. I prepare my tea, add some almond milk, and take a few minutes to enjoy it. Instead of drinking it in a rush or heading to my home office straight away, I like to sit in my meditation corner, close my eyes, and enjoy the smell, taste, and warmth of my drink. In the summer, I prefer to make some natural ice tea, a smoothie, or a juice. I repeat the ritual of touching and smelling all the ingredients and actually taking my time to drink my "morning power drink".

Sometimes on weekends, I like to prepare some take away tea and just go for a short walk. Again, it depends on your time. But you can always close your eyes and enjoy your morning drink, because you deserve it.

Tip #7 Your Mind Loves Mindfulness. Give It a Natural High!

Just like you need to wake up your body, you also need to wake up your mind. What I really recommend are vision boards and positive reminders that you always see around your house or work place. It doesn't have to be big. For example, you can have your mini vision board in your wallet or in your phone. The concept is to have a few minutes a day where you can just dream in a mindful way and focus on your vision. Let's say that one of your elements in your vision board is creating wealth and abundance. Maybe you want to have a summer house with a pool? Focus on it for a few minutes. You can even do it while mindfully sipping on your morning drink. How would it feel to have a swim in your own pool? Feel the sunshine on your skin, smell the sun lotion and ...feel relaxed.

Besides, dreaming and having a vision, even if your goals are unrealistic for the time being, will help you move forward and be excited. It will help you be more creative and productive. It's good to know where you're going even if you still don't know exactly how to get there. However, your body and mind are alert. They are mindful and ready to work for you. Your wish is their command!

Tip #8 Mindfulness and Positivity Through Journaling

I heard about journaling a few years ago but to be honest, I only developed a regular practice last year. Before it was on and off. I would reject it saying that it wasn't for me. You see, I like activities that involve being in movement, and since I sit a lot when working in my office, I somehow believed that sitting down to journal could be a waste of time. I was wrong. Now I only wish I had gotten started on it years ago. I think it could have saved me many sad and anxious moments and transform good into bad. You see, journaling is a great mindfulness practice, and you can do it anywhere. The most important thing is to see what works for you. Some people like to journal first thing in the morning, just after getting up. I personally prefer to wake up my body first and then sit down and journal. I like journaling before I start planning my day because my thoughts are much more organized and thanks to being more mindful, I get a realistic grasp of what I can do in one day. Before, I would create endless to-do lists and feel angry with myself because I couldn't find enough hours in the day to do all of those tasks. Thanks to journaling, I was able to make a stronger connection with my inner energy, intuition, and also my vision.

Mindfulness is also about realizing, understanding, and reminding yourself of your vision and focusing on where you're going, not where you're coming from. This simple mindset change will help you feel as if you had much more time in your life.

I always get asked what I write about in my journal and the best way to go about doing it. Let me tell you this- whatever you feel is right for you is your best way of doing things. I can give you a few ideas, but in the end, it's all up to you. Simply create a new mindful habit of journaling for 5 minutes a day. It can do real wonders and the more you do it, the more you'll feel like doing it. This will be something you will look forward to so much that you won't be tempted to oversleep. This is topic for another book- most people sleep too much, or too little!

Back to journaling... Focus on your emotions and how you feel now. Be honest with yourself. Write it down. Maybe you have something on your mind. Then, write down that you are in control and you can change how you feel. Create a series of positive reminders. These can even be some random words and expressions, for example: smile, inspire other people, here and now, focus, I am grateful... Remember to relax and breathe. It's your sacred journal and your writing. It's all up to you.

You can also write down your goals and your vision for life. You may also add today's goals and this week's goals.

For example: *I feel a bit tired today. This is why I will add more fresh fruits and vegetables into my diet. My main focus today is my health. Instead of going overboard with my phone and e-mail, I will breathe and stretch whenever I get a chance.*

You can also write down your ideal state:

I am full of energy and vibrant health. I look like a yoga teacher... I eat healthy and I love it...

These are just a few basic ideas to help you get started. One thing is for sure- journaling and mindfulness go hand in hand. It's all about talking to yourself and developing self-love and self-awareness.

Tip #9 Mindful Planning Without Over- Planning

Ok, I have already mentioned to-do lists. I love planning and being proactive. However, I have noticed that I feel happier and more productive if I also allow some time and space for the unexpected. Sometimes, things just crop up and there is no reason to try to be a superhero and use your lunch break or sleeping/recovery time to cross everything off of your to-do list. Also, if you follow my morning ritual tips and my journaling tip, you will feel more focused and more connected with the here and now. This is why you will be able to choose the most important things. Things that actually help you get closer to your goals. Not things that just keep you busy, because everyone is busy. Now, I am not talking about getting lazy or postponing things. This is not a "mañana" thing. What I am saying is that you need to be a bit selective. Doing things in a mindful way may also mean saying no to certain things. Also, sometimes, you may not be physically able to get everything done, even the things that are important.

Accept it. Analyze it and think what you need to change: your attitude, your strategy? Or maybe you need to give yourself some more time? Again, the more you practice the tips from this book, the more focus you will get and finally, you will embrace new levels of productivity, where mindful relaxation is also extremely helpful. For now, just keep reading with an open mind and think about what you can start applying now.

Tip #10 Mindful Affirmations

Affirmations are your soldiers and they can help you win as many battles as you want. The world can be full of distractions and negativity. However, you as a mindful warrior know that the best way is to dive into positive stuff. When I first heard about affirmations I thought it was a hippie dippie thing. I did not even feel like calling it a self-help tool. Now I can only regret it. Whenever you feel like you get off the healthy and mindful track, call your soldiers and create your powerful affirmations.

Use them to your advantage. Here are some examples:

- *I control how I feel*
- *I create my life*
- *I love setting new goals and achieving them*
- *I love getting up early*
- *I practice mindfulness as much as I can, it helps me get stronger*

My tip to you is that it's not enough just to mumble these things out. Make sure you use all your physiology. Smile. Relax your soldiers. Breathe in and out deeply. Imagine you are on your dream vacation. You can feel relaxed now. Now, move forward with your affirmations. Say them aloud and observe your body and mind. I am sure you will feel like doing more and more.

Most people choose to indulge in negative emotions and circumstances.

However, you choose to do things your own way. You are mindfully creating the script of your own destiny. This is why you choose to do things that some people may not be willing to do.

Affirmations may seem to be useless when you first begin with them. At least that is what I used to think. Still, I decided to follow my mentor's advice and utilized affirmations as much as I could, especially when I would notice some inner blocks or limiting beliefs.

I decided to forget all about, "I can't" and replace it with the more powerful, "I choose," "I want," and did it in a mindful and believing way. Give it a try. Keep going and you will finally start to notice how mindful affirmations start changing you from the inside out. You will also realize that the changes are coming from a deeper level. This is because you will be able to communicate with your sub conscious mind and re-program yourself. It may take time and work. All you need to focus on right now is to:

1. Believe in it

2. Observe your thoughts and emotions

3. Pick up all negative patters

4. Create powerful affirmations to transform them

I believe in you. Now you need to believe in yourself. And give it a go.

Tip #11 Mindful Natural High Moments

You probably heard about all this Law of Attraction stuff and how feeling good can help you attract good things. LoA would be a topic for another book, but let me just say that I personally believe in a solid balance that you can create between the Law of Attraction as well as something that I call the Law of Action. In my humble opinion, all successful people take massive action: however, they do it from the viewpoint of confidence and good feelings.

Many people may disagree by saying that I am getting way too philosophical and what I am saying is not real. Fair enough, I will respect everyone's opinion. As long as your beliefs help you move forward and live well, go for them. As long as they do not hurt other people. Stick with them. However, the problem is that many people reject new, and actually much more empowering, ways of living before they have tried them.

What I suggest in this mindful tip is to focus on the positive and search for meaning behind whatever it is that you do. Why do you get up and go to work or school, or why do you take care of your kids and take them to school?

Whatever it is that you do daily, whether it be your regular activities to put food on the table or maybe getting an education and being successful, why do you do it?

Whenever you get a chance, get a piece of paper and pen (for some reason I prefer to do this exercise in an old-fashioned way so I avoid technology devices) and try to find as many *why's* behind whatever it is that you do as possible. Of course, one of them will be making money and financial success. It is quite obvious. In fact it is so obvious that there is no reason to put it on your list (unless you want to). Most people, when asked why they work, say that they need money to pay the rent, mortgage, car etc.

Take a few deep breaths and go deep inside your own mind. How does your work activity make you a better and stronger person?

Think about it, most people are victims of a pattern that says:

"I will be happier when I change my job", or "I will be happier when my business is successful."

It's like going into a bar and reading a sign that says: *free drinks tomorrow.*

The problem is that tomorrow never comes.

However, you can be happy right now. You are on your way. Besides, some people are always unhappy, and it's because they are always looking for something and they never appreciate what they already have.

To be honest, I feel really happy because I do what I love. However, in order to achieve it I had to do things I did not really enjoy. And even now, having a business I am really passionate about, I still need to learn to be prepared for setbacks and some mind numbing tasks that I don't always enjoy. However, I focus on the bigger picture and so should you.

A few years ago I was in a job I did not like. Still, after a while I actually enjoyed going there, even though I had to commute 1 hour to get there. I remember that most employees of that company would complain about work and how their salaries were never enough. Yet all they could focus on was having some drinks after work. It's not that they had a plan or something.

But there was one exception. There was a girl that was always at peace and happy. I asked her, "How can you be so happy and relaxed if you hate this job?" She said, "I am just being mindful. I won't be here forever. However, there are also many good things going on. For example, I get a chance to meet some people like you! I don't see the point of complaining. When you complain, it makes you feel weaker, not stronger. When you try to come up with reasons why you actually come here, even if you don't like it at first, your attitude will change. Besides, there is always something new you can learn working for this company, even if it's not your real destiny or passion."

I decided to follow her advice. I managed to come up with more than 10 reasons why I would show up at work and actually enjoy it. I focused on trainings that the company would give me. Even though it's not my sector now, it's always good to learn new things. Instead of complaining about how I had to be up at 6 AM in order to arrive at work at 8, I decided to be happy about it. Getting up early is great, and thanks to this job, I got a chance to get used to it.

I used commuting time to listen to music, podcasts, and audiobooks. My new mantra was, "I am gonna go to work and do the best I can as if it was my dream job already."

My point is: be mindful and try to come up with at least 5 reasons of how your daily activities help you become a better and stronger person.

Back to my story- I quit that job 3 years ago and so did my colleague. Those who were complaining are still there, complaining as always. I quit the job but I managed to maintain a good relationship with the company. The world is small, you never know.

Now I am my own boss, but I still use the technique I just described. I know many self-employed people or small business owners, like me, who complain about taxes, government, clients, councils, regulations... They panic when the sales drop and feel like quitting. They lack mindfulness behind what they do. Of course, I am not judging, I have been there myself at some point. It was thanks to my old colleague, Paula, that I got inspired and gradually changed my attitude.

OK, your turn. How does your work or your activities help you become a better person? Come on, there must be something. You learn focus, hard work, determination, getting up early... Be mindful about it and appreciate the fact that your activity can contribute to your self-growth. If you reject it now, no matter what a good deal of a job or business you get later, you will eventually end up miserable and unhappy.

Why did I call this tip: natural high?

Because this is what it does. It helps your brain get on a natural high. People love to grow and feel creative and productive. You can give yourself this feeling right now. All jobs and activities are necessary in some way and every one of them can help you grow. It's not that a business owner is better than an employee or a CEO is better than a person who cleans the CEO's office.

We are all people and we all do things that are necessary.

As my late grandma used to say: all kinds of work, as long as they are honest, help you become a better and stronger person.

Tip #12 Work Routine Made Exciting and Fun

Like I have already said, you can be happy and enthusiastic about your work, even if it's still not your dream job or business. You can mindfully choose those feelings right now. Create a work routine that is exciting and fun. Even if you are currently not working and are looking for work, or starting a business- these are very important and special moments when you are actually creating something new. You are making a great effort that many people, I included, will appreciate.

By applying some of the tips from this book, you will find it much easier to get up early and create your mindful morning rituals. So don't worry if you can't do it now, it will come. This should be your main goal: do things in a different way. While most people get up grumpy, complaining, and they somehow try to stay in bed longer believing they will have more energy, they actually achieve the opposite. They cling to their beds like proverbial turtles in their shells. They get up doing things really fast and become victims of negative thinking.

The purpose of this exercise is to prevent it. Grab a pen again and write down:

My perfect morning routine

I love getting ready to go to work. I get up at (add your ideal early wake up time). I have plenty of time to take care of my mind and body.

Now write down all the details, all of your morning routine. Make sure you keep it in your wallet. Re-write and tweak it if you wish. Read it again. If you really want to, things will begin to change only after a few days. Positivity always brings back positivity. This is a really mindful morning planning.

Tip #13 Commuting or Driving to Work. What's the Stress all About?

All countries are the same. There is certain hour where all of the sudden, everyone is trying to get to or from work on time. What is this madness called? It's simple. It's lack of mindfulness. You already know that if you plan your morning in a mindful way and do your best to be at your peak state, you will actually be able to get up earlier and feel more energized.

This is why you will be able to skip the madness and head to your workplace earlier.

You can also do it when you work from home. I myself am in the early AM club (I get up at 5-6AM). When I have my first long break, it's probably around 10AM. Many people start their work while I can already say that I have done a heck of a good job and the most important things are done. This motivates me to work more and be more productive. By getting up early I manage to avoid stress and I also create more time for breaks like yoga, going for a short walk or run or making myself a vegetable juice.

To sum up - "the early bird catches the worm."

I believe it's true. Try it yourself. It can help you create more free time and wellness. Don't be like a turtle hiding in your shell, and don't oversleep.

You may find it hard now, I know. I can understand. But again, it's a lifestyle and mindset change. By becoming more and more mindful, even getting up early will be an amazing experience. Mindful people love life- every second of it. Nothing feels better than to see the world wake up and get ready for another day!

Tip #14 Mindful Short and Sweet Breaks

I know that for many people it does not seem very realistic, but productivity is not only about how many hours you can work and how much you can get done. It's also about how you feel while working. In other words- keep wellness by your side.

I believe that you are more productive when you feel physically and mentally energized as well as happy and enthusiastic. This is why I believe that taking short but regular breaks from work can do real wonders to your productivity and overall wellbeing. It does not have to be anything fancy. Long breaks can make you a bit lazy or you may forget about what you were just about to do.

This is why I am a big believer in short, mindful breaks. You may grab yourself a glass of water with lemon and enjoy the fresh citric fragrance. Say to your subconscious mind, "I am relaxing now. I am charging my batteries. Now, I am ready to go back to work again."

The key concept here is to make sure you don't accumulate tension. Think about it- if you work constantly for many hours and do things in a rush, it will be hard to unwind, even if you go to the best spa or massage studio in town. If, however, you take the mindful approach and do your best not to accumulate too much tension, you will focus better and you will be more productive in a holistic way.

Create your own mindful pomodoro-style break technique. I know that many people find it unrealistic to have breaks every 20 minutes or so. In my case, I usually take breaks every 40 minutes. You can grab your favorite drink (preaching time: keep it healthy please, and don't overdo the caffeine), stretch, or even do a few squats. You already know the trick of mindful people, right? They can take even the shortest amount of time and intensify it by embracing every split second.

Tension, too much stress, eye strain, all are now things of the past. You are mindful and you take care of your mind and body even when you are busy working hard. You can easily afford to give yourself 5 minutes every hour so that you experience mindfulness that leads you to being more holistically productive.

Also, humans were not made to sit in front of their PC's all their lives. This is against our nature. Of course, in the 21st century, this cannot be avoided. However, we can develop healthy and mindful habits to minimize the risks that office work involves.

By adapting this attitude, you may also start asking yourself mindful questions like, for example:

- Is excess social media really necessary?
- Can I spend less time in front of my PC?
- What is the most mindful and productive way of getting this project done?

As an author, I very often get asked about my writing routine. The way I see it is this. My main task is to be 100% focused on creating quality content that can help and inspire you. This is why I cannot do anything else. I can't go on a social media spree or start checking my e-mails. This will only spoil my efforts and reverberate on the quality of my work.

I apply the mindful attitude. There are certain times of day and week were I am 100% off-line. All I do is writing or coaching. When talking to a client, I don't want to be distracted by e-mails on my iPhone. This could drastically lower the quality of my services. Even if it is just for a second, my subconscious mind would start analyzing and thinking about the new information, so I would not be able to help my client.

Whatever it is that I do, I put my body, mind, and soul into it 100%.

I also plan certain times of days when all I do is to answer my e-mails, Facebook and Twitter messages. My focus is on communication, instant communication, and making sure I do a good job on that. But it's not a time when I focus on being creative or writing a new book.

Make things simple. Avoid multi-tasking and too much instant communication.

Let me give you another mindful tip. I was born in 1983, so when I was a kid there was no internet and no mobile phones. To be honest, I got my first mobile phone when I was 19 (which was when I moved out). My parents got a home internet connection when I was about 17, but I did not have my own PC, I just shared one with my brother back then. Besides, since most of my friends did not even have their e-mail accounts yet, nobody was that interested in hanging out online. We were more into going out.

Now I see kids and teens going overboard with their phones and other devices. They get addicted to instant communication that actually makes them helpless when it comes to the real world and meeting and talking to people in person or even on the phone.

When I was a kid, I would just play outside the block of apartments we lived in and my mom would just call me back from the window.

As a teenager, every Friday or Saturday I would head to a small square of my home town where some friends and I would meet up. If I wanted to get in touch with a friend or call someone like a boyfriend, or a potential boyfriend, I had to call their landline and very often talk to their parents, introduce myself and only after all that could I talk to them. Conversations would be kept brief: so, when and where are we gonna meet up? Simple.

Now, there is no end to instant communication. People talk to screens and keyboards. And in most cases, it's not important, it's not necessary, and nobody is gonna die if you don't reply straight away.

Don't get me wrong, I love technology and the internet, but in order to not go mad, I very often do technology detoxes. You may try to do it as well. You will get more focus, creativity, and peace of mind. Remember, nobody is going to die and the world is not going to end if you don't reply straight away. Also, in the old days, when I was young (I am still young, I just like to say it as a joke) people would very often call one another instead of getting glued to their keyboards. Think about it. How much instant communication can you delete from your agenda in order to gain more time for other important tasks? Of course, if your friends or family live in another country, it's cheaper to use the internet to communicate. If, however, your friend lives a 15 minute drive from you, wouldn't it be better to meet up in person or at least call them?

Keep your energy for more productive and mindful tasks. The rest can wait.

Tip #15 Work to Live, Not the Other Way Round- be Holistically Productive

A few mindful questions. Is stressing out so much really important? I know that some stress, in moderate amounts, can motivate you to move forward and it can actually be a good thing. But too much stress can be paralyzing. Do you want to start a vicious circle pattern? I agree that financial status and success can be important, I also believe in having ambitions, new goals and constant progress in all areas of your life. However, if you want to do it in a mindful way, you need to add some life and lifestyle goals in between. You also need to give your mind a break.

What has become extremely popular now, I think it's kind of a trend, is a laptop- internet kind of a business. I am all for it, by the way. It gives you the freedom of time and location. But it does not mean that your laptop will work for you. About 90% or even more people who follow this business model (I am talking about people I personally met) actually get glued to their laptops for 14 hours a day or more.

I totally understand that when you create a brand or start a new project, you may have to work harder. I am not defending laziness. What I try to defend here is mindfulness and mindful balance. I know it takes work and dedication to create any kind of a business- whether it's online, offline (underline or overline!).

The new 21st century trend of having an online business can be great, I am all for it, but it can also steal your freedom if you don't plan things. Also, don't buy the label of easy passive income. The irony here is that the way this model is advertised and marketed is: make passive income, travel. Stay on the beach. You don't need to do anything.

Well, quite honestly, I would call it: have a successful company or an automated business model. However, and this is a really big however, there is always some work to do, and if you don't grow your business, it will die. Things can be automated but not 100% passive.

Unfortunately, many people buy into this model only to realize they spend 16 hours a day on their laptops. Where is your life? Where is real life? Online or offline? Where's the freedom that the online marketing guru was talking about in this expensive program or seminar?

Believe it or not, I personally know people who pose as lifestyle design and online marketing gurus who claim they work only a few hours a week and spend the rest of their time in the gym or on the beach, but reality is actually much different. Yet they are still in front of their laptops, working actively. There is no balance, but they try to sell you the dream of balance.

Keep things simple. What is your goal? What lifestyle do you want to create? Do you still remember how good it feels to have a walk on the beach and get some fresh air?

Whatever work it is that you do- you do it for lifestyle reasons. People want abundance and wealth to live their lives and fulfill their dreams. Be mindful about today and don't postpone your life. Give your body and mind what they need.

I have provided an example of something that seems to be a trend these days (having an online business), however I want to add that I believe there is nothing wrong with working for someone else, or having a different business model. In other words- this was only an example, a metaphor, please do not take it too directly. I know people who work for companies and are more free and happy than some people I know who are their own bosses. The most important thing is to create a lifestyle that works for you. The bottom line is: do you live to work, or work to live? Do your work, or does your business provide the lifestyle that you wanted, or is it more of an obstacle Can this be fixed by focusing on what actually works for you and your business or your work and listening to your body?

As a wellness coach, I very often get approached by people who have lost touch with their bodies and minds and even though they were able to accumulate tremendous amounts of materialistic success, they feel lost and don't know how to enjoy it. One simple word- mindfulness, is the key.

Why are you here? What is the reason you work so hard? Right, so one day you want to be free. Did you know you can be free right now?

Of course, people may make different lifestyle choices and very often there are sacrifices. I myself had to make many sacrifices. However, by sticking to my mindful routine, I was able to utilize whatever little time I had and intensify it and use it to my advantage. Wellness was also my motivation. You see, my wellness lifestyle is an essential part of my business. I do not use any advertising campaigns or anything. People approach me and ask for help because they get inspired by my lifestyle and the results that I get.

Ok, enough of preaching time, my friend. You know I don't usually like to preach, so please allow me to make an exception here.

Just think about it. Be mindful about the lifestyle you want to have. 15 hour work days may be necessary to achieve it, but when will the madness end? What is the priority here?

All I am asking you is to be mindful and listen to your body. Your health will not wait and no amount of money will help you achieve wellness. Wellness is free and so is mindfulness.

By the way, I do 15 hours work days sometimes, but not every day. And whenever I choose to work for 15 hours I make sure that I also plan some mindful breaks in between. I don't want to go mad.

Tip #16 Stay Nice and Fresh

I love the phrase "feeling nice and fresh". Do you feel that way now?

If not, why not?

What would make you feeling nice and fresh now?

Maybe washing your face and neck with some nice organic essential oil scented soap? You can go ahead and do it now. You can also imagine yourself doing it now.

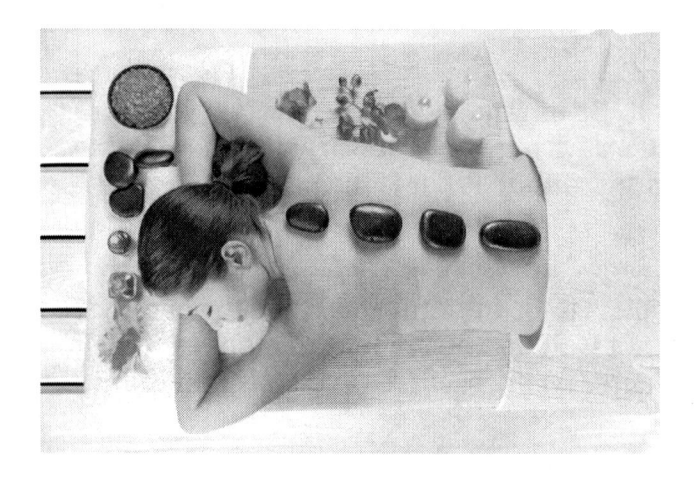

Take a few deep breaths. How does your body feel? Is there any pain and tension? Simply stand up and stretch in a mindful way. Focus and concentrate. Direct your breaths to that painful spot. Touch it with your beautiful hands.

This is your mini self-healing session. Add some mindful affirmations like: *I feel more relaxed now. Wow, that was amazing. I can't wait to do it again.*

What stops you from giving yourself those tiny healing moments? This can be done even on a busy schedule.

Tip #17 Mindful Eating

Most people eat in rush while stressing out and thinking about their next task on the old to-do list.

It's time to erase this negative habit and create something much more empowering and mindful.

I suggest you go ahead and practice it now. Grab something healthy to eat, for example a piece of fruit. Take a few deep breaths. Wash it, peel it if necessary. Put it on a nice plate in front of you and sit down if possible.

Keep breathing. Rotate your head and gently stretch. Take a piece of fruit and smell it with your eyes closed. It came from Mother Nature. Now, it's here to help you energize and revitalize. Say thank you for this gift. Many people out there don't have enough food, many nations starve. And you have this magic piece of fruit and you can also use your eating time to heal yourself from the inside out. Taste it. Enjoy it. Focus on the texture. What does it feel like? Imagine an army of nutrients and vitamins entering your cells.

Open your eyes and say thank you for this gift again.

Now, you can get back to work. You have created a health and mindfulness spa. It was only a few minutes, but you embraced and intensified those moments.

You can also do mindful cooking. Cooking and planning your meals can be really relaxing. Most people complain they don't have time. What? How can you say that? You need to feed your body and give it what it needs. This is an investment. You need to invest in yourself. Transform your kitchen into a health spa. This is your spa and your lab. Play some gentle relaxation music.

Keep everything around clean. This is not a time to stress out. This is your relaxation time, your sacred time. You create meals that support your goals and you can relax at the same time. It's also about changing your mindset.

Instead of complaining that you don't have time, start small and create something like a healthy salad. The reason why I recommended playing some music in your kitchen is that you will automatically associate the cooking process as something fun.

I actually got a bit hungry just now. And I have lots of great music and guided meditations I want to play in my kitchen. So excuse me while I have a break to mindfully feed my body and mind so that I can be back here in 10 minutes and hopefully keep inspiring you.

Why don't you go and do the same? Even a healthy herbal tea or a smoothie could be a great idea. It's your own health lab. A wellness factory. Your inner energy while creating your meals is also really important. Tune in, relax and enjoy!

Technology was supposed to help us create more and more time. Unfortunately, as more and more people get addicted to it, they actually move away from the most fundamental activities such as healthy meal preparation. Break the vicious cycle now...

Of course, I am not saying that you can't eat out or order food, there is nothing wrong with that. You can also do it in a mindful way. Go for healthy options and choose foods that support your goals. And focus on your food. Switch off your laptop, tablet, and even your mobile.

Additional Resources (Free Downloadable Audio Version Included)

www.holisticwellnessproject.com/blog/mindfulness/mindful-eating/

Tip #18 Mindful Waiting (cut off your fingers)

Sometimes there are moments that we are waiting for someone. Let's say you are in a coffee shop waiting for a friend. Before I get into this simple mindfulness tip, I want to let you know that I am not judging, as I have also been guilty of the busy fingers syndrome. Yes!

Have a look around. Most people are addicted to their mobile devices. We look like robots! It's time to stop the madness. Of course, I am not saying that you should not answer your e-mails or instant messages. All I am saying is that you should ask yourself this mindful question: is it really necessary? What am I supposed to do now? Am I supposed to be on a break and relax my body and mind? Will constantly scrolling up and down my mobile screen help me relax my muscles and my eyes?

Instead, hide your mobile in your pocket or your bag. You are in charge. You decide when you use it. Embrace the moment. Whatever or whomever it is that you are waiting for, focus on the present moment and your emotions. Do a little mindful meditation. Have a look around. Touch your neck and your forehead. It feels good to give yourself a nice soft self-massage. It feels so much better than hunching over your mobile device or tablet, right?

Besides, we need some mental breaks. You may think you are productive by using some of your waiting time to browse through your e-mail or the news, but the truth is that we only have certain amount of information we can absorb. And in this day and age we are just completely oversaturated with information.

There is also a safety issue. I see people getting entirely too focused on their mobile devices, scrolling up and down while driving. How sad is that?

I also see people having gatherings and still nervously consulting their mobile devices.

My tip is to assign certain times of the day and certain moments to your mobile phone and indulge in it. Then stop it. You are a mindful and sensitive human, not a robot, right? As a modern, 21st century individual you should use technology to your advantage, but you don't allow it use you. It's as simple as that.

Tip #19 The Best Mindfulness Drug - Music

Your mind can travel to the most exotic locations whenever you want. Use music therapy to change your mood. If you want to be relaxed, look for relaxation, spas, and meditation music. Guided meditation or even hypnosis is great for that also. If you want more energy and you don't want to end up as a caffeine addict, use songs that make you feel happy and awake. Create different playlists on your PC or mobile device. Heck, technology can be a great thing if you know how to go about it!

Music will help you switch off and energize. You can utilize your commuting and driving time. Of course, for safety reasons, don't listen to hypnosis or guided meditation whilst driving!

Tip #20 Change Your Mood with Aromas- Mindfulness Spiced Up

What comes to your mind when you hear the word aromatherapy? I am sure it's a deep sense of relaxation. The most luxurious spas in the world know that aromatherapy is the quickest way for us to relax. When exposed to natural, relaxing aromas of essential oils, it literally takes us only a few seconds to enter a more peaceful state of mind.

You can use vaporizers and diffusers to bring your favorite aromas to your workplace or home. You could also opt for an aromatherapy bath, or mix a few drops of your chosen essential oil in a tablespoon of good quality cold-pressed oil, like for example coconut oil, and go for self-massage.

I love taking mindful breaks to massage my neck. I usually choose oils like teatree, citronella, verbena, and bergamot. Citric oils help me re-energize my body and mind and fragrances like lavender help me to sleep better.

You can always find a few minutes a day for a simple aromatherapy self-massage. Experiment with different aromas. They will help you remain focused and productive. If you wish to explore this topic a bit more, you can visit my blog:

http://www.holisticwellnessproject.com/blog/natural-therapy-spa/

The most important thing is choosing your preferred aromatherapy oils and getting acquainted with possible contraindications as well.

Tip #21 Smile- It's Free!

It's normal that during the day, there are some problems that pop up and issues we need to solve. How are you going to confront them? Are you going to act from the mentality of fear, anger and self-doubt? Or from the mentality of confidence?

If you want to protect yourself from anxious states, don't forget to smile. When you smile, your whole physiology changes and you are protected. Do it now. Stand in front of the mirror and smile. Now try to smile from the deep inside you. It's not enough just to put a big grin on your face while still indulging in negative thinking. Employ your whole physiology. Smile from the bottom of your heart. Keep smiling- it looks good on you!

As you smile, observe your feelings. Breathe deeply in and out. Be proud of yourself. You are now making friends with your emotions in a truly mindful way!

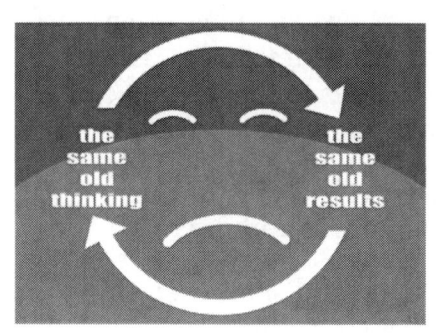

Tip #22 Mindful Holistic Self-Massage

You can always stop for a few minutes to take a few deep breaths and massage your face and head. I will guide you through this easy and really enjoyable process now. Your task is to observe the body and mind connection. Don't force anything, just let it come and observe the power of self-touch.

Sometimes there is no reason to take pain killers. Many people get headaches because of muscular tension that accumulates in the forehead that is then intensified by a rather unpleasant combination of other unhealthy factors:

- Too much stress
- Too much computer work and no breaks
- No relaxation
- Unbalanced nutrition, too much caffeine and dehydration

You don't need to be a certified masseuse or a physiotherapist to simply learn to listen to your body and get rid of tension as soon as it shows up. All you need to do is to find a couple of minutes, have a mindful break, take a few deep breaths, and follow my steps:

- Close your eyes and relax your shoulders and neck

- Don't forget to breathe. Make it deep and slow, everything else can wait, it's all about you and your wellness now

- Place your hands on your eyes and keep breathing

- Now gently move your hands up to your forehead, and imagine a white light entering your head, and then radiating down your body, and returning up through your hands and entering through your forehead. That's it, and remember keep breathing deeply, you are feeling more and more relaxed with this mindful energy circle

- Now, move your hands onto your ears and enjoy the silence, finally slide them down onto your neck. You are now ready for a massage

- Place your fingers on the top of your head, thumbs on your eyebrows

- Start from the point where your eyebrows meet (the third eye). Gently press the points and do small, circular movements. Feel your forehead muscles move around and relax.

- Keep moving your thumbs following the eyebrow line. Take your time. Finally, gently circle your temples. How does it feel?

- Now, squeeze your eyebrows again.

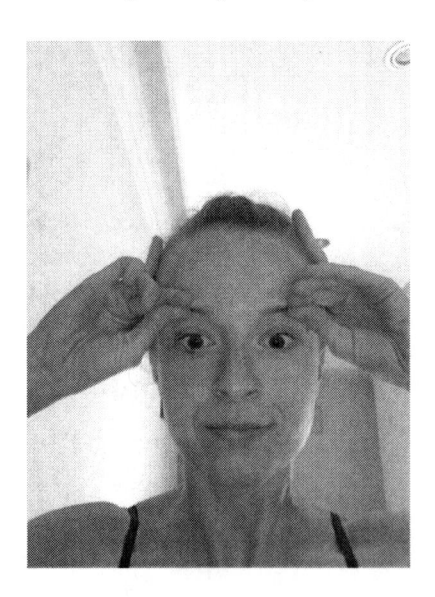

Finally, squeeze your earlobes and move your hands to the back of your head

- Using your both thumbs and the same circular-like pressing movement you have just used on your eyebrows, work on your occipital bone. By working on your pressure points in that area, you will alleviate and prevent neck pain.

- Take your time, be mindful and observe.

Trust me, a few minutes here and there will do real wonders for your wellbeing and you will be more focused and productive. What are you waiting for? Try it!

Tip #23 Mindful Anxiety Relief (solar plexus)

This very simple exercise will help you alleviate anxious feelings when they arise. Take a short break and breathe in and out. Place both of your hands on your solar plexus and while still deeply breathing in and out, observe the movement and the sensation in the palms of your beautiful hands.

Now, when you're ready, start pressing the palms of your hands against your solar plexus and gently rotate your hands. Keep breathing. How does it feel? Can you feel negativity dispersing away? Now, exhale it away. There is no place for anxious feelings and negativity. You are now ready to move forward with your active but stress-free day. You are a holistic warrior, and the holistic tools of mindfulness that you are using help you achieve your goals while remaining calm and happy.

You can also place a few drops of an essential oil mixed with vegetable carrier oil on your solar plexus. I especially recommend sweet orange, mandarin, lavender, and verbena essential oils. You can also use them to massage your feet. Mix your EO (essential oils) with good quality cold-pressed vegetable oil. Do not apply EO undiluted. While doing the massage, enjoy the sensation of essential oils. Breathe in and out. Focus on the sense of touch. You are in control because you have the tools to eliminate pain and tension naturally. All you need to do is to indulge in a few moments of mindfulness.

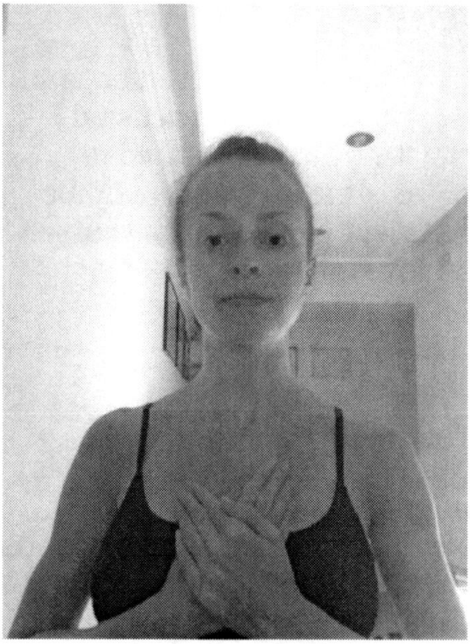

Tip #24 Mindful Communication

I must admit that what I am just about to advise you on is still a challenge for me. Well, I am not perfect, and never said I was. Mindfulness is also about self-honesty. You need to realize your weak points and try to come up with a plan. Be realistic, but also don't overdo. Accept yourself, give yourself the right doses of self-love and move forward.

So, what is my weak point?

Well, I still need to focus a bit more on listening. And this is what I do. I try to practice mindfulness while having conversations with other people. It actually helps me be more focused and nicer. I also become a better communicator and I learn to speak more slowly. I usually tell people what my weak point is and tell them to remind me to shut up. Yes!

While communicating with other people, remember to smile and listen to them and their voices. Here I refer not only to their physical voices, but their inner voices, their minds and souls. Where are they coming from? What can you do today to help them in their journey? How can you be more compassionate and listen more to what they have to say? How can you make their day better and happier?

Of course, it's much easier to practice it with people that you like and it becomes a challenge when you are faced with people you can't stand. But still, try to approach them with good energy and positive feelings. It's normal that some people put on masks of anger and negativity, but there is no reason to judge as we all fall victim to negative states at one point or another. It's just that now, we know what mindfulness is all about and since we like it and it works for us, we stick with it.

Listen to what others want to say. Breathe in all the words that come to your ears. Embrace them and understand where those who say them are coming from, and where they want to get. See it as your mission to help them get there faster and in a smooth, enjoyable way. You may not realize it yet, but there are many people out there that have the same mission as far as you are concerned. They want to help you get wherever it is that you want to get, faster. Listen to others and other will listen to you. Listening is life.

Tip #25 Create Positive Energy Around You

You don't need to tell other people that you are now practicing a more healthy mindfulness lifestyle. As long as you live it, they will feel it in a positive way. See it as your mission to create positive reminders for others. Smile and be helpful. Pay attention to other people's needs. Maybe there is an elderly person struggling with their shopping bags and you can help them?

Or maybe there is someone who seems to be somehow bitter or sad, but you can make their day just by saying something nice or paying them a compliment? Don't judge other people, very often it's not their fault that they are not polite. This is what a lack of mindfulness did to them. However, by embracing mindfulness and making it your lifestyle, you can inspire others. Believe it or not, by helping others you will feel much happier. If you look around you and become more aware of your surroundings, your energy, as well as other people's energy, you will always find a way to help others and contribute to the world. This may be as simple as inspiring those around you with nice words, a smile, or a compliment. This is positive energy creation and whether you think it's actually real or not, this very energy will come back to you.

Tip #26 How to Create Natural Caffeine Boost with Mindfulness (your mindful cup of coffee)

You already know the power of positive feelings and energy. You already know that by embracing mindfulness you can control how you feel. As Deepak Chopra says, our body has its own internal pharmacy. We don't need to resort to drugs like caffeine to stimulate it. Natural therapies and mind and body techniques can do real wonders for our health and overall wellbeing.

Instead of saying: "Oh man, I am so tired, I need another coffee," create new, more empowering beliefs and do everything you can to help your body energize itself naturally.

Take a few deep breaths. Go outside or open the windows, you need to get some oxygen. Tell your subconscious, "I am going to take a mindful break to energize my body and mind." Hop around a bit, stretch, and breathe deeply in through your nose and out through your mouth. Very often your body gets tired because of the lack of movement and dehydration. This is why a sedentary office lifestyle in front of PC supplemented by hectoliters of coffee and technology overstimulation does not help.

Do yourself a favor and energize yourself naturally. Feel the body and mind connection. Create a new mantra that says, "I feel full of energy. My body feels amazing."

It's like sending your body commands so that it works for you and pays you back with vibrant health. Create it with mindfulness first, then ask your body to work for you. When you go to bed, repeat it again, this is your mantra: "I am going to sleep now. Tomorrow I will get up early feeling full of energy!"

The bottom line is: eliminate all the, "I am so tired," or "I think I am getting old" lines. Of course, you need to take care of your body with good nutrition and you need to choose natural, unprocessed foods. You already know this if you are a health-conscious person. However, there are also other factors, and these work closely with body and mind connection. So, dive into it and talk to yourself. The more you say, "I feel tired," the more your body will feel tired.

Take advantage of mindfulness. Whenever you have a glass of water or a cup of tea, say to your subconscious, "This is my superpower elixir, it will make me feel amazing!"

Repeat with all of your meals. The more you do it, the healthier you will feel and more health you will attract. You will also want to eat healthier and will become more aware of how your food was prepared and where it came from (in case you eat out).

Tip #27 Make Things Simple (technology)

A mindful lifestyle is about creating balance and simplicity; this is why we need to redefine the role of technology in our lives. Technology should help us communicate better and faster. I think it's fantastic and I am very grateful for it. Since I left my country when I was 20, I like to keep in touch with old friends and catch up with them on Facebook. You see, this very platform was designed to keep in touch with friends and other people you know. However recently, many people use it to kill time or they get too reactive to dozens of messages and notifications. I even hear people say, "I go on Facebook on my breaks or after work." Okay, this is certainly better than getting sucked in social media while you're working, but think about it. If you were working in your office for a few hours or more, why torture your body more and keep sitting and starring at your PC or phone? If you want to have a break, go and have a break. Breathe, stretch, go outside of the building, or just walk around. Relax your eyesight and recharge your batteries like you deserve.

My mindful tip on how to use technology is very simple. Try to do technology detoxes. Simply switch everything off. For most people, Saturday, Sunday, or a holiday period is great for that. Pick what works for you. To be honest, I very often switch my phone off in the afternoon or even early afternoon. This is how I avoid distraction and over thinking as well as over replying. I also have one mobile phone for work and another for friends and family.

Have you ever tried to take a hiatus from Facebook for a week or longer? Ok, I get it, for some people a whole week may seem like an eternity. But if you just go off social media for a couple of days, and then you connect back, you will see that there was nothing that important there at all. Before you decide to go off the grid so to speak, tell your contacts that if there is something important, they can e-mail you or even call you.

A simple mindful tip: use technology to connect to people, but not to disconnect from the REAL world. There is a real life offline as well. Breathe it in and enjoy it. Your body and mind will be utterly grateful for every second of "natural lifestyle" just as they were designed to live.

Finally, it may be tempting to leave your phone on your night stand so that you can browse through e-mails and notifications before you go to sleep and you also see all this stuff first thing in the morning when you wake up. I think this is crazy. This is madness. I have been there but I decided to leave this unmindful place. If you want to maintain your mindful sanity, I really recommend you not only switch off your mobile, but also don't keep it in your bedroom. Your bedroom should be like a relaxation spa, not a mobile office. Besides, you already know the power of morning rituals. If the first thing you do in the morning is see your e-mails and messages, you might be tempted to reply straight away or, even if you don't, your mind will start thinking about them.

Again, I am not saying you should ignore important e-mails and start living like a hermit in an empty hat on top of a mountain. All I am saying is that you should try to maintain balance.

If you wish to become an early riser, you can also try to place your alarm clock (you can use your mobile) in another room, but still relatively close so that you hear it when it goes off. This will force you to actually crawl out of bed, and when you are up, you might actually decide to stay up. There won't be a temptation to switch your alarm off and postponing it while still in bed. And there won't be any temptation to browse through your e-mails and messages or other messages. Keep it simple. You already know that morning is a sacred time when your focus should be on feeding your body and mind with positive stuff so that you are at your peak state.

Tip #28 Mindfulness and Balance (How to Achieve Personal and Professional Success)

There are many definitions of balance. For some people balance equals relaxation. However, I believe that very few people have time to relax 24/7. This is why my definition of balance is a bit different. It's much more modernized. I believe that a balanced lifestyle is about employing mindfulness and talking to yourself so that you know where you're going. In other words, my definition of "mindful balance" is:

- Realize your weaknesses and fears and work on them
- Even though you are not perfect and even though you may take longer to achieve your goals, you accept yourself and you love yourself
- You want to progress in all areas of life, not just one

    Let me stop here and give you some more details. Most people, when planning their day or coming up with their goals, usually focus on their business goals. Maybe this is not your case, but I have noticed that many people focus too much on just one area of life and they neglect the rest.

    I believe that wellness and mindfulness are about working on all areas of your life, not just one. Also, there will be one area that needs more attention than others. Real balance is about being honest with yourself and thinking what you can do now, today, to make your life thrive.

When planning daily, weekly or monthly goals, I create different lists, for example:
1. Health and fitness. It's great to have one in your gym bag as well!
2. Business and finance. Be precise and keep your goals in your office, wallet, and car.
3. Education. Never stop learning, go on Udemy and grab some new courses for personal and professional development.
4. Social, lifestyle, leisure. Colorful vision boards are fantastic and so is dreaming!

If you want to get involved in mindful lifestyle design, not a mainstream lifestyle design where your only goal is to show people how much money you make, you need to have a vision for all areas of life. As long as you move forward and make progress in all of them, you achieve balance. Maybe you have neglected your health for a long time. Well, it may be a good idea to make your health and fitness goals your priority now, but of course, you should still keep an eye on your other goals, dreams, and ambitions.

Maybe, in your case, it's the other way around? Maybe you take good care of your health, but you feel like you are not satisfied with your work and the money you make? Well, then it could be a good idea to mindfully focus on your work, career, business, and financial goals. To me, health goals are as important as business goals because I know that if I feel like crap I won't be able to put my best energies into my projects. However, I also recognize the fact that if you are broke and struggling to pay the rent, no amount of green smoothies, gluten-free recipes or yoga will help. Unless of course, you decide to live on nothing or lead a sustainable lifestyle, which by the way I really respect. I know some people who live as happy hippies in the local mountains and I am also happy for them. Success is about living the life that you want.

It's all about becoming mindful about your life and make your own choices. I always say that success is about achieving your own goals, not someone else's goals. There are plenty of mindful lifestyle designs and all you need to do is to create your balance and see what works for you. Allow yourself some space for failure and testing as well. As they say, without failure there is no success, right? I wish they said this more here in Europe, but unfortunately they don't.

Now, you are ready to create your balance!

Tip #29 Fall in Love with Fitness- a Few Mindfulness Tricks That Can Help

There was a period of my life when I was working literally every day and did not really have time to go to the gym. Yet I would still go. It was like a sacred place for me, a place where I would leave my fears, worries, and anger and a place where I could overcome myself. A quick shower after a short but mindful workout, and I would leave gym feeling much more energized than when I was entering it.

At that time, I was working a lot because I wanted to save up money to study massage, nutrition, natural therapies, and other wellness related topics. I was determined to change my career and I knew what I wanted. This is why I had to make sacrifices and work overtime.

So how did I manage to be at the gym every day? It's simple. I would go just for 10-15 minutes. It's better than nothing!

That way I managed to create a really powerful habit for myself. I exercise daily, I can't survive a single day without moving my body. Fitness is life and life is fitness. If you move your body, you are grateful that you are alive and you appreciate the gift of life.

I remember that I would just go to the gym really quick, but listening to my favorite music, doings some quick spinning and then stretching would help me overcome any doubts and frustration I would sometimes face on my journey. I felt so much stronger. I remember that once, one of the guys working at the gym as a fitness instructor asked me, "Let me guess, you don't have time to stay here longer, right?"

I said, "Yes. That's correct, but at least I make it for 15 minutes. That's all I can do now."

The guy said, "Well done. Most people prefer to say they don't have time and stay at home and indulge in excuses." This motivated me to carry on. Now this extremely busy period of my life is over. I learned that if you are committed, you will find a way to keep fit.

You can always find 10-15 minutes to work out. Maybe you are not a gym type of person, I get that. Some people like outdoor activities. Think about cycling, a short run or even an energetic walk. You can also create your own workouts to do at home or even in your office.

Move your body and do it with a big smile on your face. Feel the sweat on your skin. You are eliminating toxins and negativity. You are also getting rid of emotional toxins. Mindful fitness is not only about weight loss or looking ripped. It helps you get mentally and emotionally stronger. Think about it, many people want to change the world and do incredible things. Okay, that's great. But if they can't even motivate themselves to go to the gym and work on their bodies, how can they expect to help other people change their lives?

Do your research, pick up a few tips from really successful people. The best entrepreneurs, motivational speakers, leaders, investors, authors, and thinkers are also fitness addicts. They know the body and mind connection.

Do it now. Move your body. What are you waiting for? Feel the energy, feel the movement, your life is now. Live it, embrace it and enjoy it!

Tip #30 Your Holistic Health Spa at Home and Mindfulness

I have already mentioned technology detox, aromatherapy, and self-massage. Now I want to encourage you to combine them all and create your holistic mindfulness spa at home. Plan a day, or even a morning or evening, when you will just switch everything off. While disconnecting technology and all the distractions, you will internally connect with the Universal energy that will supercharge your body and mind. Now it's only about you and your home spa.

Play some gentle, relaxing music, burn aromatherapy candles or incense sticks. Mediate, breathe, and stretch. You may also use an acupuncture mat. Treat yourself to herbal infusions, smoothies, or fresh vegetable juices. Create a healthy menu for that day. You may even want to plan to cook in advance. If you need to sleep, sleep. If this is what your body needs, this is what it needs to work for you at the optimal levels. Breathe, meditate. Enjoy showers and aromatherapy baths. Lay down on your sofa or bed, wrapped up in warm towels. It's your time. Pamper your face with natural facial masks. I know that most men will object to it, rejecting it as not very masculine, but hey- it's really relaxing. Feel the mask on your face. It relaxes your facial muscles and hydrates your cells.

Want to take it to the next level? Look for guided meditations, healing meditations, and even some hypnosis recordings. You can never relax enough.

Many people may think that taking a day off is a waste of time. But think about it, when you feel great and are at your optimal energy levels, you attract the same. Just like you need to take care of your car, you also need to take care of your body and mind.

I have just covered some basics, enough for you to get started on your holistic spa at home, but if you are looking for more ideas, or are attracted to this concept, I recommend you check out my blog:

www.holisticwellnessproject.com/blog/natural-therapy-spa/

Nature is a great healer, so you may also put it on your total wellness day or holistic home spa agenda.

Tip #31 Go Out and Have Fun- How to Practice Mindfulness In a Night Club

This is an extra tip for those who are looking for some entertainment. When talking about night clubs, or music festivals, most people would assume that that there is also drinking and even some substance use involved.

Well, people make different choices. But not all people that go out necessarily drink or do drugs, right? What I want to propose to you, especially if you like music, going out, and dancing, is to try to go out just to dance and talk to new people, but refuse drinking. If you take care of your body and mind during the day and make sure you enter the club at your peak state, you can easily get into it without drinking.

Mindfulness will get you on a natural high. Laugh, dance, and enjoy the music. Drink juices and soft drinks. When the time is right, whenever you feel like it's bed time for you, just go home. Obviously there will be many people out there still dancing and having a good time and probably looking for an after party, but since you are using all-natural energy, you need to listen to your body. Your body will provide you with all kinds of natural substances you need to have a good time.

As one of my old party friends from London used to say, "If you go to a nightclub, and you don't drink, you actually get quite a few hours of free exercise and it's more fun than joining gym classes!"

Think about it. People usually drink or use drugs because they want to relax, or they want to stay awake, or they want to feel more confident. But there are many natural ways to achieve those states and make them permanent, like a permanent natural high. Mindfulness is one of those therapies, and now you are practicing it. It will always be there for you! And it's not boring, it can even take you to a night club, concert, festival, or any music event that you enjoy.

Tip #32 Mindfulness and Self-Healing

Whenever you feel in pain, you get a headache, or simply feel under the weather, use mindful thinking. Sit down, take a few deep breaths, and say to yourself:

"Even though I feel pain now, it's gradually disappearing. Every second I breathe in and out, the pain goes away."

Of course, I am not saying that you can just sit down and talk to yourself about the pain disappearing and never see your doctor again. All I am saying is that you should see mindfulness and the body-mind connection as an additional natural tool that can help you stimulate self-healing. Many doctors would agree that patients who cultivate a positive outlook in life and take a holistic approach are much stronger. So what is the holistic way?

When you experience some kind of physical pain or discomfort, employ your mind. Instead of saying, "Oh man, I feel horrible", say something like,

"Even though I don't feel as I would love to feel today, I am making steady progress towards my recovery. I am going to explore my body and my connection and speak to my subconscious mind. It knows I want to feel amazing, and I deserve vibrant health."

Self-healing is something intuitive. I think we were born with this skill. I talk about it in detail in my book on Reiki, but to make it simple, I think that as long as you put the intention in the right place and mindfully talk to your body so that it heals itself, your recovery will go faster.

Do this short exercise. Imagine that for a few days or weeks, you are on your own in this amazing hut in the mountains. There is enough of food there so you don't need to worry about anything. There is no technology and no distractions. It's only you, your shelter, and nature. There is a crystal clear lake where you can swim and friendly animals that protect you.

All you need to do is heal yourself. What would you do? What would be your instinct? You would probably spend the whole day breathing, stretching, observing the nature and healing yourself. If you felt a pain in your neck, you would sat down by the lake and put your hand on your neck while breathing in and out. Think about it. How does it feel?

You can embrace this feeling now. Sit down and visualize your hut, your shelter where you go to heal your body and mind. Go deeper and deeper.

Tip #33 Mindfulness and Goal Setting (Mindful Vision)

When setting up your goals, you need to visualize, taste, touch, and feel all the details. Maybe you are not a visual person, that's fine. You can use other senses. If your goal is an exotic vacation, you can go to YouTube and play some sounds of the ocean. Imagine wading out into the water and having a swim. All your muscles are beginning to feel so relaxed. You can feel the salty water on your skin. Then, you go to spa in a luxurious resort where you're staying. You get pampered with massages and drink a coconut smoothie. How does it feel?

Think about other goals. Love, health, lifestyle, work, abundance. Mindfully employ all your senses. Stick to what works for you. If you are a visual person- visualize. If you are an auditory person- try to hear it. Mindfulness can help you set your goals in a really powerful way. Mindfulness will make your dreams reality and it will give you a firm sensation that you can achieve it.

Tip #34 Mindfulness and Motivation

Having problems getting motivated? First of all ask yourself why. What is it that you want and why you are struggling to take action with it?

Let's take physical fitness as an example. Close your eyes and take a few deep breaths. Now, imagine you are taking a post-workout shower. You gave everything you could at the gym and you really deserve it. You can feel all your muscles, all the cells of your body. You use a gentle scrub, then you can feel the soft towel all over your body, and you apply a natural, energizing lotion. Your muscles are firm. You are all ripped and you look athletic. You get dressed, and you are wearing exactly what you want. You feel energized, almost ecstatic. As you leave the gym, someone says to you, "Wow, you look great, your actions and your healthy body really motivate me."

Keep breathing in and out. Now...get your gym bag ready. You need your own actions, and so does the world. You will feel so much better. Besides...think about the after workout shower. You will feel nice, fresh and...mindful. Enjoy every second of it. Embrace it, this is life!

Let me give you another example. You can't get motivated to work on your new project, or study. Take a few deep breaths. Close your eyes. Imagine wealth and abundance that your hard work and determination will give you. You get up early in the morning feeling grateful, there is not even the slightest sign of worry. You have everything you need. You get dressed wearing exactly what you want. Then you get in your dream car and shop around, looking for items that you and your family want. You go online and book a vacation for yourself and your loved ones. Then you go to a local charity and you make a donation. They say, "Thank you so much, I don't know what we would do without you."

Keep the feeling. Open your eyes. Can you still afford to say that you are not motivated? You have all the motivation and perseverance you need. You never stop creating your dream life and there are no limits. There are people out there who need your hard work and dedication. So keep going, make it mindful, and move forward.

Tip #35 Mindfulness and Self-Coaching Questions

What are you doing and why?

It's time to explore the power of self-talk. A simple self-talk when you are honest with yourself but you don't judge, you only observe. You give yourself a certain amount of self-love but you don't go overboard.

Whenever you get a chance, ask yourself a few simple questions:

What am I doing right now? Why am I doing it? How does it make me feel? What can I do to make it feel amazing?

An example:

"I am driving to work. I have to do it because I need money to support myself. I feel fine, I have a job, but I am a bit annoyed because of the traffic."

Carry on:

"Hmm…I could try to have a few deep breaths and focus more on what I am doing right now. I could feel a smile on my face. I could try to be a motivator for those who are also getting annoyed at the traffic. I could use this time to calm my mind. I could be more grateful for handy inventions such as cars. Someone put lots of hard work into it and had to persevere. I can do it as well! "

Whenever you notice that there are any negative feelings accumulating in your mind, ask yourself: *why*. As soon as you have your *why*, you will know your *how*. First, accept it, don't be angry with yourself ("Heck I wanted to practice mindfulness and be positive and there we go again!"). Then, say, "Hold on, even though I give myself permission to be transparent and have all kinds of thoughts, I control how I feel. Now I decide to get rid of negativity. I decide to choose something nice and positive to think about!"

Don't force it, just let it come. Mindfulness is not about losing grasp of reality and trying to be positive with an artificial smile on your face. Mindfulness is about going deep inside, connecting with yourself and your sub consciousness and exploring. Finally, it's about observing and accepting. Only from there you can make changes that last.

Tip #36 Your Evening/ Night Ritual

Do you have an evening ritual? If not, it's time to change that. If yes, maybe you can tweak it. You already know how technology can be a distraction and you already got my advice on switching off your mobile and other devices in the evening. Of course, it's up to you. You can try it and mindfully observe how it works for you.

Here are some tips on how you can transform your evening and prepare your body and mind for a well-deserved, rejuvenating sleep...

If you want to plan your agenda, food, and clothes for the next day, go ahead and do it now. When all your planning is done, it will be time to gradually switch off your mind. Think about it as a light that gradually fades out.

Take a few deep breaths. Stand up and stretch. Imagine you're a cat. They are masters of relaxation and mindfulness. There's so much to learn from them!

Say to yourself, "I had an amazing day. I did my best to live it to the fullest. I feel utterly motivated to do the same tomorrow. This is why I choose to give my body what it needs. I am going to relax now and get ready for a well-deserved sleep."

Walk around your bedroom with bare feet. Feel the touch of the floor or the carpet. Close your eyes and say to yourself, "I am so sleepy. I am going to sleep like a baby and have sweet dreams. Tomorrow, I am going to get up feeling free of worry and energized to move forward."

It's all about having energy to move forward, right?

If you want to take it to the next level, use essential oils like lavender or verbena. You can use a vaporizer, a diffuser, or place a couple of drops under your pillows. You can also dilute a few drops in a good quality vegetable or nut oil and massage your neck, solar plexus, and feet. Create your own rituals.

Finally, when in bed, feel the freshness of the blankets and sheets. It feels so good to be protected by them. Now, feeling utterly grateful for what you have, you will snooze off…Enjoy!

Tip #37 Breathe and Just Be Yourself

Simple mindfulness tip: whenever you get a chance, breathe. Simply be, breathe, and observe. There is no reason to do any fancy meditations unless you want to. Simple methods are the best. Do it now. Close your eyes and just breathe. I am going to do the same here in my office.

Tune in. Hear the noises around you. In my case I can hear my laptop and some dogs barking in the background. I don't do anything to change it. I listen to it. I accept it.

Really, wherever you are now- close your eyes, breathe, and observe. Don't even think, "How long do I have to do this?" Switch off your intellectual mind. Think, "I will be doing this for as long as I need to and feel that I need to..."

Scan your body from head to toe. If you feel any tension, physical or emotional, breathe in deeper and deeper. Direct your breath to where the tension is. If you feel tired, just be, breathe, and observe. Whatever you do, whatever feels right for you, go for it.

Tip #38 Mindfulness and Nature

A couple of years ago, I decided to leave the city and now I live just a 2 minute walk from beautiful woods and hills. I really enjoy walking around nature and my usual habit is to listen to podcasts to absorb some information at the same time. On the other hand, when I go to the gym or for a run, I listen to music, something with an energetic beat.

Anyway, back to nature. I recently thought: how about just going for a short walk and not listening to anything? I left my mobile at home. I just went for a short walk, looking around and listening to the sounds of nature. It was amazing and so much inspiration to listen to. Try it. Mindfulness is also about changing your usual way of doing things and exploring new ways. Of course, I still love listening to motivational and informational podcasts while having my nature walks or even lying on the beach. I love going to the beach, I should do it more often now that I think about it. But I also allow myself to listen to the universal sounds of nature. They are free, always have been and always will be. Their wisdom will never end.

Tip #39 Be Like a Little Kid

Simple exercise- imagine you are a kid. Yes, a little kid! Feel the excitement. Touch everything, smell everything, ask questions and sing.

Most people will say you're mad. Who cares? I think that happiness and excitement is no crime. So feel free to indulge in those amazing feelings! If you find it hard, observe little kids and learn from them. Talk to them, ask them questions and share their enthusiasm. Children are really good mindfulness teachers, because they are real and natural.

As we grow, we put on masks to fit into society and those masks take our mindful habits away. Luckilly, by making a decision to embark on a journey of wellness, spirituality and personal development, we can get rid of masks and have unlimited levels of natural happiness. Sound good?

Explore the little kid inside you. Jump around and be curious about life. There is so much to discover.

Conclusion

Congratulations for reading this book until the very last page. I hope you enjoyed it as much as I enjoyed every second of writing it for you.

Don't forget to grab your free audio books!

DOWNLOAD LINK:

www.holisticwellnessproject.com/mindfulness-audiobook/giveaway.html

As an added bonus, I will also send you a free copy of my book "Holistically Productive" (PDF and MOBI formats).

As I bring this book to an end, I wish all these, from my heart to yours:

May you notice that you are blessed with so much.

May you notice that you are loved.

May you notice that you are happy.

May you notice that you are beautiful.

May you notice that you are kind.

May you notice that you are wise.

May you notice that you are perfect.

May you notice that the Divine is in you.

May you notice that you are alive.

Let go of your destination and enjoy your journey in life!

I wish you holistic happiness and success,

Marta

One more thing- I need your help!

If you enjoyed this book, could you please rank it on Amazon and post a short review? It will take less than a minute of your time and will be a GREAT HELP for me.

I am always happy to receive feedback from my readers. It's you I am writing for and I want to provide as much value as I possibly can. Your honest review will help me create more inspirational books for you and your loved ones. Whenever I get a review, it puts me in a positive state! To be honest, I get excited and I jump around with joy like a little kid. I read all reviews I get daily. They always make my day and help me understand how my books can be of a better service to you, the Reader! Thanks in advance. I am really looking forward to reading your feedback soon.

If you happen to have any questions, suggestions or doubts or you believe that there are some quality issues, please e-mail me at:

info@holisticwellnessproject.com

You can also e-mail me just to say hi. I will get back to you as soon as I can and I will answer all your questions. I am here to help you.

To check out more of my books and articles (wellness, health, personal development, spirituality, spa, natural therapy, healthy recipes, alkaline diet, raw foods and much much more), please visit:

www.amazon.com/author/mtuchowska

www.holisticwellnessproject.com

Finally, I would love to keep in touch with you for years to come!

Let's connect:

www.facebook.com/HolisticWellnessProject

www.udemy.com/u/martatuchowska

www.pinterest.com/MartaWellness

www.plus.google.com/+MartaTuchowska

www.twitter.com/Marta_Wellness

www.linkedin.com/in/MartaTuchowska

www.goodreads.com/author/show/7520321.Marta_Tuchowska

PHOTO CREDITS

All photos from this book were either purchased from Shutterstock.com and DollarPhotoClub.com or come from author's private collection and may not be used nor distributed in any form.

CPSIA information can be obtained at www.ICGtesting.com
Printed in the USA
LVOW06s2340041115

461105LV00027B/1152/P